The State and Government Employee Unions in France

COMPARATIVE STUDIES IN PUBLIC EMPLOYMENT
LABOR RELATIONS

The State
and Government Employee Unions
in France

FREDERIC MEYERS

UNIVERSITY OF CALIFORNIA, LOS ANGELES

ANN ARBOR

INSTITUTE OF LABOR AND INDUSTRIAL RELATIONS

THE UNIVERSITY OF MICHIGAN—WAYNE STATE UNIVERSITY

1971

This monograph is one of a series prepared under the direction of Professors Russell A. Smith and Charles M. Rehmus of The University of Michigan, and is a part of their comparative international study of labor relations in public employment. Financial support of this research project has been derived from a number of sources. Basic grants came from the comparative law research funds of The University of Michigan Law School; the Institute of Labor and Industrial Relations, The University of Michigan—Wayne State University; the comparative economics research funds of The University of Michigan Economics Department; and the research programs of the New York State Public Employment Relations Board and the United States Department of Labor.

Contents

The State and Government Employee Unions in France

·I·

The French Industrial Relations System

FRANCE has had a lawful trade union movement since 1884, when a statute affirmatively defined the right to organize.[1] Therefore, though there were trade unions, their existence and activity were threatened by the doctrine that they constituted criminal conspiracies under older law.

Like many continental labor movements, the French was, in its origins, strongly anarcho-syndicalist in its ideological orientation. This meant use of the strike weapon not as a device to lead to a binding collective agreement, but rather as a warning to the employer to improve conditions of work and as an exercise in worker militancy toward the ultimate aim of a general strike and direct worker control of each individual place of work. Collective bargaining was regarded as an inadmissible form of class collaboration. Though this characterized the movement generally, there were within it individual unions more oriented toward the present and jobs.

The first great French confederation—the Confédération Générale du Travail (C.G.T.)—was organized in 1895. At its congress in Amiens in 1906 it adopted a charter expressing the principles of independence with respect to political parties and devotion to industrial action as the means toward its revolutionary goals.

Revolutionary syndicalism and anarchism gradually became diluted by more contemporary socialism, though the principle of neutrality with respect to political parties was never formally

1. For a good general description and brief history of the French labor movement, see Val R. Lorwin, *The French Labor Movement,* Cambridge, Harvard University Press, 1954. See also J.-D. Reynaud, *Les Syndicats en France,* Paris, Colin, 1963; Maurice Labi, *La Grande division des travailleurs,* Paris, Editions Ouvrières, 1964; Annie Kriegel, *La Croissance de la C.G.T.,* Paris, Mouton, 1966; Gérard Adam, *La C.F.T.C., 1940-1958,* Paris, Colin, 1964; Georges Lefranc, *Le Mouvement syndical,* Paris, Payot, 1969; Antoine Prost, *La C.G.T. à l'Epoque du Front Populaire,* Paris, Colin, 1964.

abrogated. Following the failure of the international socialist movement to take effective antiwar action before World War I, Léon Jouhaux, the leader of C.G.T., collaborated closely with the government in the prosecution of the war. This collaboration and the worldwide split in the socialist movement occasioned by the Russian Revolution led in France as elsewhere to a split in the labor movement, with those sympathetic to communism splitting off to form the Confédération Générale du Travail Unifiée (C.G.T.U.). C.G.T.U. remained a minority movement until reunification in 1936 under the Popular Front.

A major incident of the Popular Front period was the Matignon Agreement between organized French employers, the reunified labor movement, and the government of Léon Blum that affirmed the right to bargain collectively. This led to a great wave of organization and the first, though abortive, wave of collective agreements in France on anything like a general scale. Collective bargaining practices had been limited to very few industries and employers before 1936. But the fall of the Popular Front government, internal struggles in the labor movement occasioned by international events, and the onset of the war reversed the trends begun in 1936. Little remained either of the growth of the trade union movement or of the beginnings of collective bargaining.

Unity of the Resistance papered over doctrinal differences in the labor movement, and cooperation among some groups weakened employer influence. The immediate postwar period saw a great resurgence of trade union strength within the unified C.G.T. But the second great worldwide split in the labor movement was reflected in France, after the capture of a majority of the executive board of C.G.T. by communists and their political allies, by the withdrawal of a substantial though minority fraction to organize the Confédération Générale du Travail-Force Ouvrière (C.G.T.-F.O., or F.O.). C.G.T. had affiliated with the World Federation of Trade Unions on its organization after the war. F.O. affiliated with the predominantly social democratic International Confederation of Free Trade Unions.

There had been for many years in France a relatively

unimportant Catholic labor movement, founded originally on doctrines of Catholic social action and anti-Marxism. The confederation in which these unions were grouped, Confédération Française des Travailleurs Chrétiens (C.F.T.C.), was affiliated to the International Federation of Christian Trade Unions. During the postwar period C.F.T.C. gradually became less dogmatically clerical and increasingly militant and pragmatic. As a consequence, it gained considerable strength and began to rival F.O. as the second confederation in membership and working-class influence. In 1964 it "laicized" completely and changed its name to the Confédération Française Democratique du Travail (C.F.D.T.). A small minority in this split on the issue of laicization, and continued under the old C.F.T.C. name.

A fourth confederation presently active, the Confédération Générale des Cadres (C.G.C.), has organized principally managers, supervisors, and, generally, higher level white-collar and professional employees. It is politically neutral.

The constitution of the Fourth Republic enshrined in its preamble the right to strike, and a law of 1950 provided a legislative base for collective bargaining. The 1950 law encouraged the negotiation of regional or national agreements between employer associations and the "most representative unions." Federations affiliated to the major confederations are, by definition, "most representative," and occasionally autonomous unions gain representative status.

The principle of exclusive representation is unknown in France, and compulsory unionism is illegal, although it is practiced in at least one industry, newspaper printing. Hence employers must deal with a multiplicity of unions. Since French unions are organized universally on an industry basis, usual negotiations entail possible participation of at least three and often four (the fourth being C.G.C.). However, not all unions at all times choose actually to participate actively. Some may withdraw, usually for political or competitive reasons. Nevertheless, agreement is possible, and the refraining unions may later choose to "adhere," that is, add their signatures. French agreements do not contain a no-strike clause, and unions, signatory or not, may strike during the term of an agreement, whose substantive clauses are merely minima for the industry and are of indefinite term. Only political strikes and certain strike tactics fall outside the constitutional guarantee of the right to strike.

Agreements concluded under the law of 1950 to be eligible for extension must include certain compulsory subject matter listed in the law, and may include other optional clauses. Once an industry agreement has been reached, firm or plant agreements may supplement them, though the number of such supplementary plant agreements is small. In the absence of an industry agreement, firm or plant agreements may cover only wage matters.

Provided they meet certain conditions of form, industry agreements may be extended by decree so as to cover firms not represented by the negotiating employer association. Most employees in the private sector are covered by collective agreements, usually extended. Most of these are national industry-wide agreements, though the important metal industries are covered by a network of regional agreements, not extended. However, the minimum standards, at least as to wages, are usually significantly below the wages actually paid.[2]

French law plays a major role in determining conditions of employment. A minimum wage law probably influences wages as much or more than collective agreements, directly at the lowest level, and indirectly through adjustments in the wage hierarchy as minimum wages are changed periodically.[3] Minimum vacations, now four weeks, are set by law, though the precedent was set by collective agreement. Hours of work are regulated by legislation. There is complex legislation affecting various kinds of leaves, hiring practices, etc. The law provides for a system of family allowances, which for families with children are major elements in their income. A form of health insurance is provided for by compulsory membership in a series of health funds whose

2. See F. Meyers, "Deux aspects du role des négociations collectives en France," *Sociologie du travail,* Jan.-Mar. 1965, April-June 1965.
3. Ibid.

management, by members and employers, is closely regulated by government. However, the major system of unemployment insurance is provided for in an extended collective agreement negotiated by the umbrella employer confederation and the major union confederations.[4]

Apart from the public service—the subject of the main body of this paper—terms of employment in most of nationalized industry are covered by specific statute. These include the coal mines, railroads, gas and electricity, and metropolitan transit. In these the relation of organized employees to the state-employer resembles more closely that in the public than in the private sector. A special procedure integrating the unions into decisions concerning distribution of money increases had been established for the nationalized industries, but was abandoned in June 1968.

In addition to the industries wholly nationalized, the state owns or controls certain individual enterprises, in industries in which private firms coexist, the most notable of which is the Renault automobile firm. These are operated by autonomous corporations which bargain collectively under the law of 1951. Plant agreements at Renault have often set major patterns and led to legislation.

In addition to the law of 1951 concerning collective bargaining, French law requires that in each plant other than the smallest there be an elected works council, composed of members elected principally from lists proposed by the unions. It has very limited powers, and serves principally as a consultative body. Employer hostility has kept most of the works councils relatively unimportant. However, that hostility has been softened greatly in very recent years.

Further, the law requires that there be elected, again from lists proposed by the unions, certain employee representatives whose duty is principally to assist individual employees with complaints or grievances. These representatives, once elected, are not responsible to the unions; indeed, they are obligated to represent workers who may belong to unions other than that from whose list they were elected. French employers,

4. Ibid.

however, have been extremely reluctant to recognize any formal union activity at the plant level. However, recent legislation has given union officials certain rights to access and activity at the plant level.

Disputes of right, arising out of the individual contract of employment and derived either directly from it or indirectly from the collective agreement or from the law, are dealt with by plant representatives of the workers or of the union. In addition, workers have access for this type of dispute to a system of bipartite labor courts whose members are elected by employers and workers. Appeals from labor court decisions go to the "social sections" of the ordinary appellate courts.[5]

French unions are relatively weak in numbers. Membership is hard to define, much less measure. It is as much subjective as objective; many workers regard themselves as union members though they may pay dues only sporadically. Their evidence of membership is in following union strike calls, or in voting for the slate of candidates proposed by their union to office as works council member or personnel representative. But the total proportion of eligibles who are at least usually dues-paying members has been estimated at about 15 percent in the private sector and 40 percent in the public sector.[6] Of these perhaps 60 percent are in C.G.T.-affiliated unions. C.G.T. gets more than a majority of votes for its candidates to works councils.[7]

French unions are also weak as measured by the result of their collective bargaining activity; their influence on terms of employment except in a very few industries and plants is not great. The latter weakness is accountable for in part by the tradition of the French labor movement which places much greater stress on some kind of revolutionary

5. See W. H. McPherson and F. Meyers, *The French Labor Courts: Judgment by Peers,* Champaign, University of Illinois, Institute of Labor and Industrial Relations, 1966.

6. See Michel Crozier, *Le Monde des employés du bureau,* Paris, Seuil, 1965, p. 56.

7. See Y. Delamotte, "Les Elections aux comités d'entreprise, 1967," *Revue française des affaires sociales,* Oct.-Dec. 1968.

change. By its oldest tradition it was anarcho-syndicalist. More recently socialism, both communist and more nearly social democratic, have played a major role in French union ideology. Though the French labor movement has maintained, at least formally, its tradition, dating back to 1906, of independence from political parties, political action of various forms occupies much of its attention. However, F.O. and, particularly, C.F.D.T. are moving toward concentration on job problems and direct work-related activities.

But despite its apparent weakness, the French labor movement plays a significant role in French life. It is recognized by society as spokesman for a class interest. Its representatives are given seats on the Economic and Social Council, an important advisory body to the government, in the various planning agencies and elsewhere where, as is common in France, representatives of various interest groups serve. In crisis situations it seems to have great influence over workers. Union-sponsored strikes were among the more important factors in protecting the government against a coup d'état sponsored by army elements over the Algerian War settlement.[8] Intervention of C.G.T. played a major role in termination of the disturbances and strikes of May and June 1968. In fact, C.G.T., though communist led, is frequently accused of conservatism within French society. For many purposes C.F.D.T. may have passed it on the left; C.F.D.T. certainly had more sympathy with the student revolutionaries than did C.G.T. which tried to protect workers against the infection of excessive leftism.

In general, the French labor movement may be in the process of greater integration into French society, though that process is slow. Many of the revolutionary slogans seem tired; more of the activity is pragmatic and directed toward shorter-term goals, either by dealing with employers or by legislation. Strikes are still short, terminating before goals are won and serving more as warnings than as decisive weapons. But, though political strikes still are occasionally called, their ends are more often job-oriented. They remain short because of weakness rather than in principle. Longer strikes lasting until economic goals are achieved are at least somewhat more common; witness the coal miners strike of March 1963, which lasted five weeks even after requisition, that is, effective military-like draft, was invoked. Many of the strikes of 1968 lasted for many weeks.

The process of transformation is slow, but it can be observed. Weakness is still characteristic, but the consequences of superficial weakness became less at least in crisis.

This is the labor movement of which public worker unions are an integral part. Though public employee unions are stronger in membership and richer in funds, they partake of many of the characteristics of the general French labor movement. But, as we shall see, there are differences in characteristics of the unions, and great differences in their relations to their employers, as must be the case when the employer is the state.

·II·

The Structure of
Public Employment .

THERE are in France about 2 million civilian government employees, constituting about 10 percent of the labor force.[1] This figure excludes employees of nationalized industries. Though the proportion of the labor force employed by government is not significantly different than in the United States, the distribution between employees of the national government and those of local units of government is greatly different, reflecting the greater centralization of the governmental function in France. Of the 2 million employees, only about one fourth are employed by local units of government, principally municipalities or communes. The departments have as chief executive the prefect, named and employed by the national government. Many public employees functioning at the departmental level are also employed by the national government.

These figures give a slightly deceptive view of the degree of centralization of governmental function in France. Nearly one half of the employees of the national government are in the Ministry of Education and include virtually all the personnel of the public system of education, which, in France, is the responsibility of the national government.[2] Hence, for other functions of government, concentration at the national level is a little less pronounced than is indicated by the gross relationships of numbers of employees.

Apart from education, the largest single group of public employees is that of the Ministry of Post, Telephone, and Telegraph, which numbers over a quarter of a million. Table I below indicates the distribution among the several ministries and services.

1. G. Mignot and P. D'Orsay, *La Machine administrative,* Paris, Seuil, 1968, p. 8.
2. A very few largely part-time vocational educational programs are operated at the local level. There are also some few private institutions which may receive a public subsidy.

Table I

Public Employees, by Service, in France, 1967
(in thousands)

Foreign Affairs	11
Labor, Public Health, and Veterans	25
Education	616
Post, Telephone, and Telegraph	278
Finance and Economic Affairs	126
Interior	82
Public Works and Transport	74
Agriculture	20
Justice	23
Construction	7
Civilian Personnel of the Military	149
Local Units of Government	550

Source: Mignot and D'Orsay, *La Machine administrative,* p. 8.

In interpreting these data, it should be borne in mind that two services, Telephone and Telegraph and Radio and Television, operated privately in the United States, are operated by ministries of the national government; employees in these activities are included among those of the relevant ministry. On the other hand, nationalized industries such as railroads, electricity and gas, and coal mines are operated by what are in effect government corporations. Though they may be responsible to a ministry, their employees are not included in Table I.

If the figures on their face are mildly deceptive as to the degree of concentration at the federal level, they conceal the fact that the autonomy of local units of government as to personnel matters is severely limited. Until 1920 the communes had virtually complete autonomy as to personnel matters. In 1920 the national government enacted a model statute governing the general outlines of personnel policy for the communes. Unless each commune adopted its own statute, the model automatically became applicable. In 1953 a compulsory statute, which defines the general terms of employment policies, was enacted applicable to all communes. It has been revised and amended from time to time. While it does not specify scales, it defines relationships for many jobs.

Further, salary scales adopted by the communes must be submitted to the departmental prefect for approval and may not exceed the scales for national government personnel. At this writing, a law is under consideration in Parlement, supported by the trade unions of public employees and promised as part of the negotiations during the "events" of May-June 1968 by the government. It would make the salary scales set for national government employees compulsorily applicable to the communes.

There are several categories of public servants in France. Again, excluded from consideration here are employees of publicly owned firms, such as the Renault automobile enterprise, as well as those of nationalized industries, except, as we have noted, for the government-operated television, telegraph, and telephone and postal systems.

In the categories listed in Table I, however, public servants may be established, that is hold something resembling civil service status in the United States in that their tenure is protected and that they are looked upon officially as career employees.[3] Second, there are several kinds of nontenure, nonpermanent employees: auxiliary and temporary personnel and certain personnel sometimes described as "contractual" though their relationship to the state is legally different from the private law contractual relationship between employer and employee. Further, prospective true civil servants pass through a probationary period. These categories exist both for central government personnel and for those of local units of government. Of the approximately 2 million local and central government civilian personnel, about half are civil servants in the narrow sense of the term.[4] For the nonpermanent personnel there are, however, regulations which more or less carefully define their terms of employment.

The basic structure of the civil service as well as the terms of employment is determined by the General Civil

3. Strictly speaking, these are employees subject either to the General Civil Service Statutes for Central Government Personnel or the General Statute for Personnel of Communes. These provide, among other things, for tenure.
4. Mignot and D'Orsay, *La Machine administrative*, p. 6.

Service Statute and implementing special statutes and decrees. A similar general statute enacted by the national government determines the basic structure of local government civil services and that of governmentally owned or controlled hospital and medical institutions. The basic structures are substantially the same.

Career civil servants, in either local or central government service, enter the service in a "corps." The corps group civil servants are, in principle, subject to a common special statute applying with more specificity to them the rules of the general statute. With a very few exceptions, each corps is limited to positions within a single ministry and service. Each contains a hierarchy of positions in one or more "grades." These grades are all within one of the four grades or "categories": A, B, C, or D. In general, these categories depend upon the level of qualifications required for the entry positions. Though it is not entirely exact to describe them this way, in general, recruitment into a corps in category A requires a university degree or its equivalent; into category B a secondary school diploma; into categories C and D a primary school certificate.

Each corps describes a normal career for a civil servant. It tells him what normal salary advances he may expect while within each grade or rank. It tells him what higher ranks he may normally aspire to, and what the relationship of his likely terminal grade and salary is to that at which he begins.

As has been indicated, with few exceptions, the corps is limited to a particular service within a ministry. The entering civil servant can expect to remain in that service for the duration of his career. The major exception is the corps of high level administrators, which is interministerial. The philosophy, and with few exceptions the reality, of the French civil service is that it is chosen as a career early in life, that there is little or no mobility into it from outside except at entry levels, little or no movement out of it into the private sector, except very occasionally at high levels and for certain technicians, and extremely little mobility from corps to corps within it. On entering, the young civil servant has made a virtually binding choice of a career, with known and defined limits.

Concurrently with the enactment of the General Civil Service Statute, a basic salary "grill" was established which assigned to each position title in the civil service an index number range which defined its proportionate relationship to all others. As of June 1969 the index for the lowest beginning job was 115; for the top of the grill it was 770. These indexes are for basic salaries net of taxes, and pension and medical care insurance contributions. A very few of the highest level positions may go above scale. The minima and maxima for category D are 115 and 180; for category C 158 and 308; for category B 197 and 337; for Category A 273 and 770.

The number of positions in each corps and in each grade within each corps is determined as part of the budget-making process. Entry into the civil service, both local and national, is by competition, usually involving a written examination for corps within categories A and B. Advancement within a grade is normally dependent on length of service. Advancement from one grade to a higher one within a corps is either by examination or, more ordinarily, by the selection of superior officers from among civil servants requesting that they be placed on an advancement table. As we shall see subsequently, employee committees on which unions are represented play a major role in this last procedure.

Given the commitment to public employment and to a particular corps within public employment made by an entering civil servant, his major preoccupation is with matters which concern his "career." The career is defined simply as the span of salary, status defined by a corps, and the expected number of years within each step in each echelon and grade. He is, of course, concerned with the general wage changes that are made with each budget in each fiscal year. But of at least equal and perhaps greater importance is the matter of placement of positions within his corps in the salary grill, the number of years normally expected at each step and within each grade, the ease of movement from grade to grade, the number of openings provided for in the budget and by attrition in superior grades, the equity of merit rating procedures which determine whether he proceeds normally or more rapidly than normal, avoidance of discipline that may penalize him by deprivation of seniority equivalents, and matters of such sort.

Of less concern are matters of job security, since by rule the civil servant is almost perfectly secure. He is protected by a system of discipline committees, and more importantly by a hierarchy of administrative courts, against loss of his job for disciplinary reasons. He holds rank, rather than a specific job, and elimination of the job does not deprive him of his rank or the perquisites that go with it. Rank is formally disassociated from specific duties or positions. The elimination of a job simply means that he may be assigned to other duties, not that he risks expulsion from the civil service, demotion, or transfer to another corps. Only in the case of complete abolition of a service may his job be in jeopardy, and then only under most rare circumstances.

As the mention of entry qualifications indicate, for most positions possible entry depends upon levels of education achieved in the ordinary state school system. (There are almost no private schools in France, and none at the university level. Their curricula are controlled, in effect, by the state, since only the state can issue recognized diplomas.) However, for the elite group of higher civil servants, two of the *grandes écoles* deserve special mention. The highly elite Ecole Polytechnique, whole antecedents go back to the Napoleonic period, prepares engineers. Its graduates normally enter the public service in engineering or technical positions, but may go into corps which lead to administration of such services. The Ecole Polytechnique is administered by the army, and its graduates are obligated for a period of public service. Most remain there.

The second major institution is the Ecole Nationale d'Administration (E.N.A.), founded just after World War II. Entrance into it, as into the Ecole Polytechnique, is highly competitive and limited. Upon entry, if they were not before, the students become paid civil servants. Most entrants are from the academic secondary schools, but certain places are reserved for young civil servants. Both sets of places are filled by written and oral competitive examinations. Graduates from the E.N.A. go into the preferred ministries in the top corps or into the interministerial corps of professional administrators. Ministerial cabinets and the highest levels of the civil service contain most of the graduates of E.N.A.

·III·

The Rights of Public Employees to Bargain and Strike

PRIOR to 1946 public employees in France had neither the legal right of organization in trade unions,[1] the right of collective representation, nor the right to strike. The right to organize and join unions was limited to employees related to their employer by a contract of employment, according to decisions of the Conseil d'Etat[2] relating to the right of public employees to organize. Further, the Conseil d'Etat seemed to read into the right of organization the right to strike which, it held, was "incompatible with the essential continuity of national life."[3] Mutual associations of public employees for purposes other than dealing with the state as employer was the permissible limit of organization. Many such associations were organized under an act of 1901. As we have seen, however, unions of public employees existed from about the turn of the century. Indeed, certain governments tacitly or explicitly recognized or encouraged them as interlocutors.[4] Though the prohibition extended to employees of local units of government, they were often recognized in some sense by many communes, particularly those with left-wing local governments.[5] Formally, however, the denial of the right to

1. An act of 1884 finally established the right to organize for workers generally. Though it is not entirely clear, public employees thereafter might join unions without legal sanction, though these unions had no legal standing to represent public-employee members in court, administrative tribunals, or other formal proceedings.

2. The supreme judicial body in the hierarchy of administrative courts. It also has other functions.

3. See A. Brun and H. Galland, *Droit du travail*, Paris, Sirey, 1958, p. 652.

4. Ibid., p. 653; see also A. Tiano, *Le Traitement des functionnaires,* Paris, Génin, 1957, pp. 254, 257.

5. This statement is based on interviews with veteran trade unionists in the "Service Public," the phrase used in union circles to describe local government service.

collective representation is a corollary of the denial of the right of self-organization.

Jurisprudence of the Conseil d'Etat held that concerted cessation of work or its encouragement deprived public employees of the right of access to disciplinary remedies, save only for proof of the fact. In addition, the penal code sanctioned the act of encouraging a strike of public employees.[6] Belorgey, however, found only one case in which this penal sanction was employed.

The constitution of the Fourth Republic, however, in its preamble, guaranteed the right to strike "within the framework of laws which regulate it." This guarantee was carried over into the constitution of the Fifth Republic. No exception to this guarantee was made as to servants of the state. And until 1963 the only laws which regulated it concerned the police, certain employees of penitentiaries, and the judiciary. For these employees, strikes are forbidden. In. addition, the General Statute of 1946, establishing regulations for the civil service, explicitly established the right to organize. It was generally agreed that the constitutional protection of the right to strike applied to public as well as private employees. But as to both, judicial interpretations made the substantive content of the guarantee more precise.

Strikes by public employees are not uncommon, and usually they are short and limited to a single service or corps.[7] But they may be much broader. Civil servants participated widely in the prolonged disturbances of May and June 1968. Though political strikes are illegal, there was, of course, no prosecution against these.

First it was held that protected strikes had to have an objective related to employer-employee relations; political strikes were not protected. Second, certain forms of collective

6. See G. Belorgey, *Le Droit de la grève et les services publics,* Paris, Berger Levrault, 1964. This is an exhaustive and definitive legal treatise on the right of public employees to strike.

7. No good strike statistics for the public service seem to exist. However, see Tiano, *Le Traitement,* for lists of strikes of public employees, 1930-1957. There is no reason to suppose they have become much less frequent since 1956.

action were held not to be strikes within the meaning of the guarantee, or not protected because they were abusive exercises of a right. In this category fell such actions as slowdowns, deliberate misperformance of work, sudden strikes called before demands were presented to management, and certain other forms of work disruption. The constitutional protection was interpreted to mean that during a protected strike the individual contracts of employment were suspended. Hence the employer could not dismiss an employee for the act of striking. If he did so, the dismissal was an abusive exercise of a right and subjected the employer to liability for payment in lieu of notice and (often nominal) damages. However, an employer might lawfully dismiss a striker for improper acts during a strike, as, for example, violence, destruction of property, or interference with those who wished to work.

The general definitions of a protected strike applied to public as well as private employment. In addition, the government was held to be empowered to adopt reasonable regulations for its own employees, by administrative fiat, as if these were laws regulating strikes under the terms of the constitution, and as an exercise of the power of the sovereign to assure the continuance of vital services.[8] Such explicit regulations were enunciated in circulars of 1953, 1954, 1956, and 1969.

The circular of 1953 distinguished between employees who might participate in a strike and those who might not by their position in the salary hierarchy. The subsequent circulars abandoned this criterion, substituting a functional one. Public servants who "were possessed of a part of the public authority and whose continuing presence is indispensable to the life of the nation" were forbidden to participate in a strike. Each service was required to make up a list of such positions, notify the public servants involved, and inform them of the sanctions which might be imposed in the event they struck. Public employees who might not have the authority described,

---

8. Under a specific statute, employees in public or private enterprises might be "requisitioned," a procedure analogous to a draft into military service for the duration of the strike. See H. Sinay, *La Grève*, Paris, Dalloz, 1966, pp. 421 ff.

but whose interruption of service might endanger safety of persons or public property or the continuance of activities essential to the life of the nation, were explicitly made subject to requisition in the event of strike. In addition, the circulars required that public servants engaging in lawful strikes could not be paid for the time lost on account of a strike. Further, strikes for part of a day were to entail loss of pay for the entire day.

In 1963 a statute was enacted specifically regulating the right of public employees to strike. That law applied to persons directly employed by the national government, by departments, and by communes with a population of over ten thousand. It applied also to nationalized industries operating under statute and certain other enterprises performing a public function. The law has two major restrictions on the right tó strike. It provides that a strike is unlawful unless preceded by notice of five days given by one or more of "the union organizations most representative, nationally, occupationally or in the organization, enterprise, or service involved." This means that any union affiliated with one of the several trade union centers recognized generally as "most representative" may give notice. In addition, unions unaffiliated with such a center may legally give notice only if it is recognized in the organization, enterprise, or service as among the "most representative." An example of this latter case would be the autonomous Federation of National Education. The notice must include a statement of the objects of the strike. As Sinay remarks, this gives a monopoly to recognized unions for the purposes of conducting a lawful strike of public employees covered by the law and introduces legally for the first time in France the implicit notion of the wildcat strike.[9] It is worth noting that the purpose of the strike notice provision is not primarily to permit further negotiation or mediation—it is too short for that—but to permit preparations for safeguarding health and property and the necessary minimum of service to essential users, or to permit users to prepare.[10]

9. Sinay, *La Grève,* p. 384.
10. Ibid., p. 383.

The second restriction is the prohibition of "revolving strikes" —those in which one group of workers in an enterprise or service strikes for a short period, returns to work, and then another group walks out. And finally, the law confirms the provisions of previous circulars under which a strike for part of a day entails the loss of pay for an entire day.

Sinay believes that nonmention of other activities previously regulated by the courts leaves these doctrines unchanged. Thus strikes for objects unrelated to employment would continue to be unlawful, as would certain other forms of collective action.[11] However, highly authoritative legal sources consulted personally by the author on this problem believed grave questions have been raised as to the status of this jurisprudence after the passage of the law of 1963.

The sanctions provided for by the law for participation in an illegal strike are purely disciplinary. If the government agency imposes any sanction less than dismissal or demotion, its sole obligation is the transmittal of his personnel record to the affected participant employee, an old guarantee designed originally to protect against political notations being placed in personnel records. He loses his right of recourse to established bipartite commissions. Presumably, his only recourse to the administrative courts would be to test the fact of his participation in an illegal strike. Further, while the agency may invoke the penalties of dismissal or demotion, the affected employee, in cases of the most severe sanctions, retains his right to access to procedural remedies.

At this point it might be noted that as to the true "fonctionnaire," or person with what might be called civil service status, reinstatement is the accepted remedy for improper dismissal. This is not the case for 'the employee in the private sector who, generally, is entitled only to pay in lieu of notice and possible damages.[12] Thus a striker in the private sector may be dismissed if the employer is willing to pay the economic price, even though the strike be lawful.

11. Ibid., p. 382.
12. See F. Meyers, *Ownership of Jobs*, Los Angeles, U.C.L.A. Institute of Industrial Relations, 1964.

The government, however, must take back a striker so long as the strike was lawful.

It is highly doubtful that the provisions of the law of 1963 have had great practical effect. It depends upon the will and courage of the administration for its enforcement, either by disciplinary action or by actual withholding of pay. Interview and observation has led to considerable doubt that either is done with any frequency. Clearly, and especially since May 1968, many though not all strikes of public employees have taken place without the required notice. I have been told by officers of several public employee unions that since May 1968 their unions have, in principle, not given the required notice. Yet they are unaware of any disciplinary action against participants in the strikes.

While public employees in France have the right to strike, in the most usual sense they do not have the right to bargain collectively. That is, the government does not enter directly into binding agreements with the unions representative of its employees. Basic terms and conditions of employment, as later discussion will show, are determined by statute. Continuing discussions do go on at various levels either between trade union officialdom and the government, or between employee representatives elected from union lists of candidates or nominated on union proposition. But in general these discussions are purely advisory, or are in informal procedures. And for certain very important matters, most particularly general wage changes, the system seems almost deliberately devised to dilute the ability of unions to get binding commitments. This is a problem different than that in the United States, in which the executive may not be able to bind the revenue-producing authority, for in France both because of constitutional provision and because of the effective control of the Parlement by the government during most of the period since 1958, the government can, if it wishes, make agreements which it can consummate. The problem in France is the effectiveness of union access to decision-making power.

These matters will be amplified in a later section of this paper. But it seems appropriate here to attempt some explanation of the seeming paradox of this aspect of the French situation seen through American eyes. In the United States it has been much more difficult to establish the right to strike than to establish some reasonable approximation of the right to bargain collectively. The reverse is true in France. In the U. S., public employee unions have generally been much more insistent on the right to enter into effective bargains than to demand the statutory right to strike.

These comparisons must, of course, be qualified by the observation that increasingly U. S. unions of public employees have struck and have attempted to defend themselves against sanctions for the strike; that is, they have sought the de facto right to strike without demanding its formal expression in law.

The problem may be looked at from the perspective of the trade union movement, and from that of government. If both perspectives are put into the larger French context of industrial relations, the seeming paradox makes a great deal of sense.

From the perspective of the French trade union movement, the strike has only infrequently been a means to the end of the conclusion of a binding agreement with the employer, public or private. Apart from any class or revolutionary aims, the strike has historically been seen as a demonstration and warning to employers to change, unilaterally, some complained of condition. It has not ordinarily been conceived of as a means toward the end of a bilateral and mutually binding agreement to alter a managerial decision, in return for termination of a strike which began with the view to continuance until the reaching of such an agreement. Indeed, for a considerable part of their history, French unions viewed the conclusion of a mutually binding collective agreement as inadmissible class collaboration. As we have seen, collective bargaining, in the American sense, has not been highly developed in France. Hence to the public employee unions the importance of the right to strike lies in the ability to stage such demonstrations. It is not inextricable, as it is in the American environment, from the conclusion of collective agreements. To the French unions the right to strike is a valuable right quite apart from the right, or ability, to conclude a collective agreement. It may, indeed, be regarded as more important than the right to conclude a collective agreement.

It is partly in this setting that the government regards the meaning of the right of public employees to strike. Historically, of course, the basic constitutional document, the preamble to the constitution of the Fourth Republic, was written in the immediate postwar period when many employers and the more conservative political forces and figures were tainted with collaboration and wielded little influence. Furthermore, it is not entirely clear that its application to public employees was at the forefront of the minds of those who drafted the constitution.

But practically speaking, in endowing public employees with the right to strike, the government was not yielding that part of its sovereignty which had to do with determining unilaterally the terms upon which people would become its servants. It was only yielding that part of its sovereignty which had to do with unilateral disciplinary power. And the latter had been effectively yielded earlier; it was well understood that government's disciplinary powers over its servants were subject to what were then understood constraints. In the same year they were formalized in a statute. And, to the real constitutional casuist, sovereignty was seen as preserved in that, in legal theory, rights granted to public employees by statute survived no longer than the statute; they did not become indelible.[13] Hence the constitutional guarantee of the right to strike would be looked on simply as a guarantee that so long as the government imposed on itself disciplinary guarantees for its employees, striking within the laws which regulated it would be subject to the self-imposed disciplinary restraints.

In a much more practical sense, endowing public employees with the right to strike, given the French context, may not

13. See Roger Grégoire, *The French Civil Service,* Brussels, International Institute of Administrative Sciences, n.d., pp. 56, 76.

have seemed to present the same danger as might be the case in the U. S., of prolonged cessations of essential public services. As we have noted, it is the very rare French strike which endures to the bitter end of settlement upon agreed terms. They tend more often to be short demonstrations of a few hours, or at best a day or two. Hence to those who see all public service as essential, the likelihood of its prolonged interruption seemed less imminent than might be the case in the U. S. And in fact the device of requisition, though its use might not, in 1946, have been foreseen, is a much more drastic means of assuring resumption of service in case a prolonged stoppage is threatened than anything known in the U. S. except in wartime. (It might be remembered that the first requisition statute in France was written in anticipation of war.) It is directed at forcing the individual striker to resume service, and not merely at the unions or the strike leadership.

French unions tend to reach higher into the managerial hierarchy, both in the private and public sector, than is the case in the United States. Hence it may be more difficult to maintain skeletal essential services in the event "supervisors" respond to a strike call. But this problem has been dealt with, as has been noted, by the administrative rules which designate certain essential personnel who are required to remain on duty during a strike.

In a way, then, French regulations as to the right to strike do not express the rigidity of the notions of sovereignty as do many others which regard as inappropriate any yielding of the sovereign power to discipline employees. But furthermore they express perhaps a more realistic view that not all public services and personnel are equally essential. The personnel of certain services are denied the right to strike: police, the judiciary, and penitentiary personnel. For other services distinctions are made between positions as to their essentiality. Such distinctions no doubt assume that a public employee strike is likely to be the typical stoppage of short duration. Requisition, which might well be unconstitutional in peacetime in the U. S., remains for the serious and prolonged strike.

The problem of the right to bargain collectively seems further from solution in France than in the United States. Yet there is less pressure from the unions to deal effectively with this issue since U. S. style collective bargaining is, not only in the public service but in private employment as well, less central to the function of the labor movement. This does not say that unions are not concerned with conditions of employment; only that there is not the determination to influence them by way of similar institutional arrangements.

·IV·

Trade Unions in the
Public Service

UNLIKE the case of the United States, unions of public employees in France have a long history. Furthermore, for most of that history, including the present, public employees have been more effectively organized than employees in the private sector, at least as measured by the ratio of actual to potential membership.

The earliest substantial unions of public employees were associations of postal employees organized around the turn of the twentieth century.[1] These had been preceded by mutual aid societies organized under an act of 1884. The associations of the period after 1901 were organized under a law of that year permitting associations of public employees for the study and defense of mutual interests. They could not, however, strike nor could they represent individual workers before tribunals, although they conducted several unsuccessful strikes in the period 1900-1910. Around the same time, primary school teachers and certain municipal workers organized into associations. The postal workers remained independent of C.G.T. in this period, though the schoolteachers affiliated in 1905.

The great wave of public employee unionism, however, came after World War I. In 1921, according to Prost, there were about 120,000 members of public worker unions affiliated either with C.G.T. or C.G.T.U., the latter a communist-dominated group which had just split off.[2] This represented

1. See Alain Plantey, *Traité pratique de la fonction publique,* Paris, Librairie Générale de Droit et Jurisprudence, 1963, I, 100. For brief accounts of the history of public employee unionism in France, see Tiano, *Le Traitement,* ch. VI; M. Crozier, *Le Monde des employés de bureau,* Paris, Seuil, 1965, ch. III. Most of the general histories, of course, contain references to public employee unions. There are several studies, of uneven quality, of particular unions.

2. Prost, *La C.G.T. à l'époque du Front Populaire,* p. 200. The figures appear to be based on membership for voting purposes at the Confedera-

about 15 percent of the total membership of unions in the two federations. Of the total, about two thirds was in public employee unions affiliated to the old C.G.T. The big unions were in the postal service and among employees of local governments. The figures do not include the large unions of teachers and central government employees which were, in 1921, independent. In 1926 these independent unions had affiliated,[3] and total membership in C.G.T. and C.G.T.U. unions of public employees had grown to more than a quarter of a million, nearly 30 percent of the total membership. Furthermore, union membership seems to have been about 30 percent of total full-time public employees in this period.[4]

Crozier estimated that in 1932 the three largest unions of public employees—teachers, postal workers, and central government civil servants—had 35 percent of the total membership of C.G.T.[5] After the great wave of unionism in the mid-thirties, the total membership of public employee unions, according to Prost, reached more than 500,000 out of a total union membership of 4 million in 1937.[6] Despite the fact that private sector unionism increased in this period more rapidly than that in the public sector, the latter, with about 50 percent of its potential in unions, was still in 1937 the more heavily organized.

Unfortunately, data as good as those compiled by Prost, Kriegel, and Labi for the period from 1911 to 1937 do not exist for the post-1937 period, but the general patterns established up to then seem generally to have prevailed since.

---

tion congresses. Public employees appear to be more regular dues payers than members of most other unions. This appears if Prost's figures are compared with those in M. Labi, *La Grande division des travailleurs,* Paris, Editions Ouvrières, 1964, p. 248. Labi's figures purport to be based on membership paying dues 12 months of the year.

3. According to Grégoire, the C.G.T. was fearful of the influence of a large block of nonmanual workers with the corporate interests of civil servants, and delayed the admission of the Civil Servants Federation until it agreed to break up into six directly affiliated federations. See Grégoire, *The French Civil Service,* p. 58.

4. See Mignot and D'Orsay, *La Machine administrative,* for some historical data on the number of public employees.

5. Crozier, *Le Monde des employés,* p. 51.

6. *La C.G.T.,* p. 200.

Those patterns indicate that public sector unionism is, at least in terms of membership, stronger, more stable, and more consistently growing than that in the private sector.

In the immediate post-World War II period, there was a great expansion in trade union membership, comparable to that of the period of the Popular Front. Public as well as private employees participated in that growth, though proportionately less rapidly, if for no other than the statistical reason that it was already better organized, though the hiatus of the war and occupation interrupted the life of French trade unions. But in the decline of the latter forties and early fifties, public employee unions maintained their strength better than did the rest of the movement.

The schism of 1948, of course, affected unions in the public sector as well as those in the private. The most important effect was the decision of the powerful Fédération de l'Education Nationale, the teachers union, to withdraw from C.G.T., now dominated by communists, and to remain unaffiliated rather than to belong either to C.G.T. or to the new C.T.F.-F.O. The other public employee unions split. By 1954, by which time the situation had stabilized, F.O. and C.G.T. appeared to be almost equal, at least as measured by votes in elections to bipartite commissions. Excluding teachers, each gained about one third of the vote, the balance going to C.F.T.C. and autonomous unions.[7] In terms of occupational structure, however, the C.G.T. public employee unions probably had more of the people in the lower level, manual and manual-related occupations, while F.O. unions attracted more members among the middle and upper level civil servants. C.F.D.T. (and the antecedent C.F.T.C.) has only recently begun to develop strength in the public sector.

Crozier estimated[8] that, by 1965, 40 percent of public employees belonged to unions, compared to about 15 percent of employees in the private sector. These estimates correspond quite closely with those given to me by well-informed French observers. The best organized sectors are teachers, postal

7. Tiano, *Le Traitement,* pp. 261-62.
8. *Le Monde des employés,* p. 56.

workers, and municipal employees. The strongest public employee union is that of education personnel, the autonomous F.E.N., with an estimated 80 percent of its jurisdiction organized.

During the period from the schism until the present, C.G.T. probably gained strength slowly relative to F.O. Precise relative membership figures are not available, nor are even reasonably good estimates. But some measure of relative loyalties of public employees can be obtained from results of elections held for various bipartite commissions in the public service. Recent compilations have not been made public by the director of the civil service. However, a study done by Gérard Adam[9] in 1967 indicates that, excluding teachers, candidates of slates of C.G.T. received about 40 percent of the votes, F.O. about 30 percent, C.F.D.T. about 15 percent, the C.F.T.C. (Sauty)[10] about 5 percent, and the balance were, except for a very small number going to candidates of the C.G.C.,[11] for candidates of unaffiliated organizations. Both these, and official figures for the 1963-66 period cited in the Adam article,[12] would indicate that by 1966 or 1967 C.G.T. commanded the voting loyalties of more public servants than did F.O., though the official data showed the C.G.T. lead to be substantially narrower. Adam interprets the difference to result from the placement of "common lists." Several years earlier, C.F.D.T. would not have made such a large showing. The study was made shortly after the affiliation to it of a certain large autonomous union in the Water and Timber Service of the Ministry of Agriculture.

Adam's study shows F.O. to be the larger vote-getter in civil service categories A and B, while C.G.T. is the leader

9. "La Représentativité des organisations syndicales," *Revue française de science politique,* April 1968.
10. At the time of the "deconfessionalisation" of C.F.T.C., a small recalcitrant group led by Joseph Sauty of the Miners formed a confederation with the old C.F.T.C. name.
11. A politically neutral confederation of "cadres," that is, upper level white-collar, professional, and supervisory or managerial workers.
12. See also *Le Monde,* Dec. 29, 1968. The report then of the official figures indicates that although F.O. got fewer total votes than C.G.T., it won more individual seats.

in categories C and D; that is, in general F.O. was more successful in retaining its strength among office and upper level civil servants, C.G.T. among those closer to manual status.

The structure of trade unionism consists generally of federations or national unions with jurisdiction by ministry or service. The Fédération de l'Education Nationale has, for all practical purposes, no competition in representation of teachers and other personnel in the educational institutions. It is a federation of national "syndicats" or unions whose jurisdiction in turn is divided according to the level of education: the big national unions are those for primary school personnel, secondary school personnel, and higher education.

For both F.O. and C.G.T. there is an affiliated federation with jurisdiction over municipal employees and those of hospitals and other health institutions. In both there is some internal administrative division between services for health employees and for municipal employees. Local unions are organized by commune and by health establishment.

Similarly for both F.O. and C.G.T. there is a federation of federations for central government employees, excluding, in both cases, postal, telephone, and telegraph workers. The subordinate federations, or in some cases national "syndicats," are organized by ministry. In some instances, local or national unions divide manual from nonmanual workers. Affiliated directly both to F.O. and to C.G.T. is a Federation of Postal, Telephone, and Telegraph Workers. The structure of unions of public workers affiliated to C.F.D.T. follows essentially the same pattern except that the postal workers are in the general federation of civil servants.

It should be noted that C.G.C., the confederation of supervisors, technicians, and upper level white-collar workers, has a federation with some small public employee membership.

For national bargaining purposes, formal or informal "cartels" of the three big federations—municipal workers, postal workers, and general civil servants—are formed for each of the confederations. For many purposes, however, the federations are autonomous. As will be noted later, most of the important national bargaining for municipal workers is with the central government, which retains great authority over the municipalities in personnel matters. Hence the municipal employee unions participate in the bargaining cartels with the unions of central government civil servants.

Public employee unionism has occupied a somewhat anomalous place in the French trade union movement. It has been consistently stronger and more stable than the predominantly manual worker unions in the private sector. In part this may be explained by the lesser fear of retaliation by a hostile employer, even in the period when public employee trade unions occupied a dubious legal position and were denied the right to strike. This is especially true of municipal worker unions in those communes in which socialist or other left-wing local administrations not only tolerated but encouraged unionism. In part it is attributable to the structure of mutual benefits tied directly or indirectly to trade union membership. These are quite old and reminiscent of the efforts of A.F.L. unions in the U. S. to achieve membership stability in this way.

The French trade union movement has been, for most of its history, a class movement, and this fact, combined with the lesser risk, may help account for the early attachment to trade unions of public employees having manual jobs or likely to come from manual worker families: postal workers, sewage and sanitation workers in municipalities and others. Yet teachers were among the early groups among public employees to form relatively strong unions. There was, undoubtedly, among many such intellectuals a strong sense of ideological identification with working-class movements.

Despite these facts, in general public employee unions have been on the political right of the French labor movement. This is evidenced by the much larger proportion of public employees who left C.G.T. to form F.O. in the 1948 schism. F.E.N., though not joining F.O., left C.G.T. for autonomy. C.G.T. suspicion of public employee unions in the twenties is evidenced by the admission conditions which diluted the political strength of civil servant unions in the Confederation. The leadership of C.G.T. civil servant unions talked to me about the "political backwardness" of their membership.

One might have supposed that with their strength and

stability the public employee unions might have wielded greater political strength in the movement to keep it further to the right, at least prior to the decision of substantial numbers of them to leave with F.O. Only two hypothetical explanations can be advanced here. The first is that the leadership, always anxious to prove their allegiance to a working-class movement and their place in it, were reticent to assert political leadership over manual worker unions. The second is that the membership, more concerned with corporate problems, turned inward and was inherently less anxious to play a leadership role in the wider movement. So long as they were left to deal with their problems, they cared little about the political directions of the confederations to which their federations belonged. And, until the schism, the slogan of unity was sufficient to prevent rebellion.

·V·

Trade Unions and Basic Terms of Employment

THE basic terms of the employment of civil servants, both local and national, are determined by a set of statutory documents enacted at the national level. As to national civil servants, the two basic documents were adopted in 1946: the General Civil Service Statute and the salary "grill." The first lays down basic employment principles: methods of recruitment, promotion, merit rating, security of employment, the system of "corps." It further provides for the enactment of implementing statutes for each of the corps. The second is a complex system of what amounts to a job evaluation for the positions in the civil service, with salary indexes for each step within each grade or rank within a corps, and provision for normal amounts of time in each step. A similar general statute was enacted by the national government for municipal employees in 1953 and for hospital employees in 1955.

The General Civil Service Statute of 1946 was regarded as a great trade union victory. One of its principal authors was Maurice Thorez, a leader of the Communist Party, then minister of state in the first De Gaulle government. Prior to 1946 a series of special laws, custom, and jurisprudence determined the rights and duties of civil servants. Though the new statute merely codified some of these older practices, it made many much more explicit, added certain privileges, provided for a structure of bipartite bodies, and made explicit the right of civil servants to join unions and to strike.

In a very real sense, the statute of 1946 was agreed legislation in whose framing the trade union movement played a major role. It also expressed the distrust of the labor movement generally, and public employee unions in particular, in a continuing process of collective bargaining. Rather than leave many matters open to continuing discussion and change, it froze as many as possible into a statute passed at a politically propitious moment. It did leave to further process of political negotiation the implementation of the general principles to the conditions of the specific corps. These and other changes not affecting the fundamental law of the statute may be enacted by the government by decree without the necessity of parliamentary assent.

Matters affecting the budget do have to go to Parlement, but, as we shall see, even there the Parlement has become less important. On most matters, then, the unions, insofar as they have effective access to the government, deal directly with the real decision makers. And while extensive consultative procedures are provided through the bipartite Higher Council of the Civil Service (Conseil Supérieur de la Fonction Publique— C.S.F.P.), effectiveness of access is impaired by the series of vetoes available at the several steps of the procedure to invoke change.

In part the eagerness of the public employee unions to accept this system may have been an expression of weakness, though it was fully in the tradition of the movement. Despite their relative numerical strength, public service unions may have felt that they could get more, dependably, this way rather than to leave the way open to easier frequent change by procedures more nearly resembling collective bargaining.

It is perhaps of significance that the strongest of the public employee unions, the teachers, have not pressed for a special statute for their corps. Despite the mandatory provisions of the general statute, no special statutes exist for educational institutions. Leaders of the F.E.N. told me that they felt they were less bound without a statute than they would be with one; that they could more easily choose their time and interlocutor when they chose to raise issues and problems. This is, they say, particularly true on matters which would ordinarily go to the bipartite bodies established for the corps with special statutes to deal with individual or organizational matters. Such bodies have not been established in the educational institutions.[1] C.G.T. leaders have expressed the goal of transforming the system into one of collective bargaining, though precisely what is meant is not clear. This would be contrary to their earlier positions.

Basic conditions of employment, then, for civil servants in France are determined by statute or decree, both for national government employees and for municipal civil servants. Furthermore, it is the national government which determines, by statute or decree, basic terms for municipal as well as national civil servants. These terms are incorporated in the General Civil Service Statutes for civil servants at both levels, and by the special statutes applying the general statutes to the several corps. In addition, there are special statutes dealing with pensions and health protection.

As to money terms of employment, the power of Parlement in budget matters has been greatly reduced. Article 40 of the constitution of the Fifth Republic, sometimes called the "law of the maximum," forbids Parlement from passing amendments to the government budget which would have the effect either of increasing charges or decreasing revenues. Hence the role of Parlement in budget matters is relatively minor, and lobbying activities of unions intended to increase salaries or other costs above those proposed by the government in its budget are largely futile. This had been a major activity of French public service unions in the interwar years.

Any influence the unions may hope to exercise so far as general wage changes, then, must be exerted on the government during the preparation of annual budgets. The budget will normally fix a percentage of general increase in salaries of civil servants. Informal or unofficial consultations are often had between trade union representatives and the prime minister, the minister of finance and his director of the budget, and the director general of the civil service during the annual preparation of the budget. These consultations cannot readily

1. A number of student, faculty, and administrative bodies have been established under the educational reforms of 1968. But these deal essentially with matters of educational policy, not with terms of employment.

be described as negotiations; rather, they are the presentation of demands by the unions. They are often preceded by short demonstration strikes. From both sides of the table there is agreement that such demands normally have little direct effect. The historic procedure seems to be that the government decides for itself, with little regard for trade union positions, what it is willing to include in the budget in the way of general wage increases for civil servants. Normally these are modest with respect to the hopes or expectations of those affected and with respect to general wage movements (including wage drift) in the economy. Over a period of two or three years, discontent builds up, finally to an explosion of strikes and unrest, leading to a major readjustment in civil service compensation. Such catch-up adjustments have occurred periodically at three to five year intervals. What happens here, however, may not be grossly unlike what happens in the private sector.

The last such major explosion occurred in the spring of 1968, when, in connection with the events of that spring sparked off by student demonstrations, civil servants got wage adjustments averaging 14 percent. Large numbers of civil servants participated in the widespread strikes, and some real negotiations took place between the government and the civil service unions. At those negotiations the government agreed to the very large general increase, and to the general principles of its distribution, particularly that a disproportionate share should go to the "little civil servants" in the lowest categories, who received about 20 percent, as compared with about 9 percent for the upper ranks. As is the usual case, the government here was negotiating not only for national civil servants but local as well, since most municipalities use the national scale.

The more normal situation is represented by what happened the following year when, despite threats of a new "confrontation" in March 1969, the government budget provided only for increases of 3 percent on April 1, with the possibility of supplementary increases in October. Following the adoption of the budget, some real negotiations took place between the unions and the director general of civil service involving distribution of the 3 percent.

BASIC TERMS OF EMPLOYMENT

Three major issues were involved in the negotiations over the distribution: how much should go to retired civil servants; distribution by categories; and the timing of increases. The parties had a specified total budgeted sum of money to negotiate over, and so long as they stayed within that sum, approval by the government could reasonably be assumed, though formal approval in the form of decrees implementing agreements reached had to be obtained.

The timing matter is of importance, for decisions concerning it set the floor from which the following year's adjustments are made. The 3 percent could, for example, have been allocated so as to give 1 percent for the first four months of the fiscal year, 3 percent for the next four months, and 5 percent for the final four months. Such a distribution stays within the budgeted amounts. In this process there are in fact indirect negotiations concerning the following year's adjustments, and, for this reason, the minister of finance retains approval authority. In case of disagreement between the director general and the minister of finance, the prime minister "arbitrates" the matter.

The discussions, or negotiations, which ensued the following October (1969) are of considerable interest both substantively and procedurally. Procedurally, they seemed more to resemble collective bargaining than had recently been the case except in the spring of 1968. The principle government representative in the negotiations was the minister of state in the prime minister's office, who could be presumed to speak for the government. The result was described as an agreement; it was reduced to writing and signed by the minister and representatives of the major unions in the public service, except for the C.G.T. unions which refused to sign. It provided for special increases for categories C and D ranging from 5 percent to 19 percent (in addition to such annual general increases which might take place), spread over the period 1970 to 1974. The signatory unions engaged themselves not to demand, during this period, other changes in these categories which might conflict with this overhaul of the structure for the lower wage groups.

39

These negotiations were of particular interest because they did in fact resemble real negotiations on a very difficult problem of wage structure and because of the fact that the government and the signatory unions for the first time committed themselves in writing to dispose of a set of issues for a substantial period, extending over several budgets. The refusal of C.G.T. to sign (as they refused to sign somewhat similar agreements in the nationalized gas and electricity industries) was said to be based in part on dissatisfaction with the substantive terms, but also on the long-term character of the agreement which, in its view, implicitly impaired the right to strike.

Distribution among categories is a problem which poses conflicts between groups of civil servants, and between unions representative principally of higher or lower paid groups of workers. Among the confederations, C.G.T. represents relatively more people in the lower paid groups, and F.O. more in the relatively higher. Within federations, the Post Office Workers are the large unions representing lower wage categories.

C.G.T. is sometimes accused of policies intending to destroy the hierarchy; C.G.C. is known as its stoutest defender. Informants in government say that despite its external voice, C.G.T. does not seek excessive advantage for its low wage constituency, perhaps because of its interest in attracting more members in the higher categories. C.F.D.T., though its membership is scattered through the hierarchy, for dogmatic reasons probably is the most vociferous supporter of policies designed to reduce salary differentials.

I inquired whether labor market circumstances led the government to positions on adjustments of structure, that is, whether it looked at recruitment and turnover problems as indexes to needed adjustments. I also asked whether the trade unions sought support for their demands for structure changes in such data. The answer in both cases was in the negative. The general explanation was in the isolation of the public from the private labor market. Once the initial decision is made to enter the public market, it is almost never reversed; civil servants rarely leave public for private employment. The rare occasion on which a former student of the National School of Administration (Ecole National d'Administration), the university level training institution for top level civil servants, takes private employment is the occasion for a newspaper story. The case of the postman or the stenographer in a government office seems equally rare. Furthermore, as we have noted, the structure of public employment makes it virtually impossible for the mid-career private employee to penetrate. And the status and security of public employment has, thus far at least, seemed to assure an adequate supply of entrants, except possibly in education, for certain technical specialties, and perhaps for the Post Office.

Hence negotiations over wage structure turn inwards toward notions of internal equities. The secondary school teacher is more concerned about the relation of his income to that of lieutenants in the army than to that of professionally trained people in the private sector. The postal clerk looks more toward the customs agent than to the shipping clerk in a manufacturing company.

The internal structure of public employment appears to exacerbate these "coercive comparisons." Not only is the public labor market largely isolated from the private, but the public market itself is "balkanized" into tiny fragments with little or no movement between them. Each corps is almost totally disconnected from any other in terms of mobility; each corps then tries to advantage itself. A relative loss is virtually irremediable to the individual since he cannot pass from one to another. Each then seeks to improve the possibilities of the "career" open to it, with relatively little regard for the interest of the entire civil service, at least so far as basic wage structures and progressions are concerned.

These kinds of issues, phrased though they may be in the abstract terms of defense or attack upon the hierarchy, are the meat of negotiations on distribution of wage increases so far as the categories are concerned. These matters are involved not only in application of general basic wage changes to the several categories, but also in supplemental wage items:

the amount and calculation of regional wage differentials, the determination of whether certain bonuses are to be paid as flat sums or percentages of salary, the incorporation of supplemental benefits into the basic wage so that they will be included in pension calculations. These, as much or more than issues of a percent or two in general wage changes, are the subjects of normal collective negotiations between the civil service unions and the government.

Between annual budgets, negotiations may take place in individual corps or ministries. The apparent principal subject of negotiations is changes in wage indexes associated with particular position titles, or the "indexicization" of positions not covered by the existing "grill." Such negotiations are initiated between the union and the chief administrator or personnel director of the corps. Whatever the result there, the problem must be passed up to the ministerial level. Assuming the minister will agree to a change, the matter is taken to the C.S.F.P. for its advice, and hence to the director general of the civil service. If he agrees to a change, he must get agreement from the minister of finance; disagreement between these two may be "arbitrated" by the prime minister. The change may be financed out of the existing budget, or it may be included in the usual government intrafiscal year request for supplementary funds. Substantially the same procedure is required for any other change in employment conditions, which normally requires a decree amending the special statute for the corps. The government may issue such decrees without Parlementary consent since they rarely require what may be construed to be a basic change in law. Where changes do not require additional funds, the minister of finance is not required to give his assent. Except for his concurrence, the above procedures describe what happens as to nonmoney matters. Further, on such matters the advice of the bipartite C.S.P.F., described briefly in the next section, must be sought and is given greater weight.

The key role played by the minister of finance often gives rise to the charge that the corps within his ministry receives preferred treatment.[2] As Tiano also notes, the sympathy and influence of each minister is a major factor in the success of a demand for revision of the special statute.

It is obvious that the system greatly dilutes whatever power the trade unions may have. It is extremely difficult to evaluate the influence of trade unions on wages and working conditions. Its basic outlines, and particularly the incorporation of guarantees into the General Civil Service Statute, was regarded by the trade union movement as a great victory. It came, however, at a time, under the Fourth Republic, when Parlement was much more powerful and much more subject to trade union pressure. During those years, lobbying was a major source of union achievement.[3] But the constitution of the Fifth Republic greatly weakened Parlement and strengthened the power of the government. Accompanying that change was the political ascendancy of Gaullist parties. Under contemporary circumstances it is more doubtful that union *power* is a major source of change in conditions of work, though union influence through the consultative processes may still be important in convincing the government of the desirability of certain kinds of changes.

No extensive study has been made of the impact of unions on wages of civil servants. Tiano indicates some of the methodological problems in making such a study. He does present some data for the period prior to the Fifth Republic, which compares compensation levels with a measure of union strength for certain positions in the civil service. For the few selected positions examined, there appears to be a rough correspondence between the two variables, but these data, as Tiano points out, must be treated with extreme caution.[4] Deductively, one would expect less apparent union influence during the period of the Fifth Republic.

Local governments have relatively little autonomy in personnel matters. Their basic terms of employment are set by statute.

2. See Tiano, *Le Traitement des fonctionnaires.* See also Grégoire, *The French Civil Service.*
3. See Tiano, *Le Traitement,* pp. 413 ff.
4. Ibid., pp. 436, 533.

The limits of their basic wage scales are set by the "grill" for national civil servants. Changes permitted within these limits are subject to supervision and approval by the departmental prefect, himself responsible to the minister of the interior. Only relatively minor matters are left to the discretion of local levels of government, and the major business of the unions of local government employees, so far as basic terms of employment are concerned, is with the national government. For those few small communes whose wage scales are not at the national government level, some negotiations are possible. But in general these are rural towns in which the civil servant occupies a relatively higher place in the local job hierarchy than in the large towns and cities. Even for these, national government scales are about to become compulsory. Hence apart from actions on application of the statutes, working through the bipartite commissions, the union role is in Paris rather than in the town. The same general statement may nel are within the jurisdiction of the unions of local government be made for the hospital and medical employees, whose person-employees.

·VI·

Trade Unions and
Work Problems

THOUGH French trade unions are still denied the right to bargain collectively in the usual sense of entering binding agreements affecting the basic terms of employment, they are given a large formal role in dealing with the day-to-day problems arising at the work place. That role is to be exercised through a network of bipartite bodies established under the terms of the General Civil Service Statutes for central government and for municipal employees.

The General Civil Service Statute for central government civil servants and the several special statutes applying the general statute to the corps provide for two formal systems of bipartite commissions: the Bipartite Administrative Commissions (Commissions Administratives Paritaires—C.A.P.), and the Bipartite Technical Committees (Comités Techniques Paritaires—C.T.P.). Further, a national bipartite commission, the Higher Council of the Civil Service (Conseil Supérieur de la Fonction Publique—C.S.F.P.), supervises these and plays an advisory role to the government.

The more important of the two types of commissions is the C.A.P. Under the General Civil Service Statute, it is charged with jurisdiction, usually advisory, on matters concerning individual employees. Such matters include advice to supervision on promotion matters, review of ratings, disciplinary problems and other similar kinds of issues.

A C.A.P. is required, under the statute, for each administration, service establishment, or agency covered by it. Under an implementing decree of February 1959, it is more specifically provided that a C.A.P. is to be established for each corps. The commission consists of equal numbers of representatives of the administration and of civil servants. Administration representatives are named by the minister having jurisdiction from among the upper level administrative civil servants having authority over the corps. Civil servant representatives are elected, two representatives for each grade in the corps, by proportional representation from lists presented by civil service unions or other groups. The vast majority of members are elected from lists presented by the large unions.

Generally regarded as the most important function of the C.A.P. is that of advising the administration on the matter of the "promotion table." Generally speaking, increases in salaries within a grade are determined by length of service. Each step within the grade for each job classification has established for it a normal period within step. In principle, advancement from step to step depends upon a kind of merit rating, as well as upon seniority. Interviewees indicated, however, that length of service was really far the more important criterion. However, the civil servant whose advancement might be endangered by reason of his merit rating has a right to appeal to the C.A.P. for a review of the rating. Further, provision is made for crediting to a limited number of civil servants in each corps seniority equivalents for good performance. This also is done with advice of the C.A.P. It should be noted also that a permissible form of discipline is the deprivation of specified periods of seniority for advancement purposes.

The more important matter, however, than advancement within grade is the passage from one grade to the next. The budget determines the number of positions available in each corps, and the proportion at each grade is fixed. Advancement from grade to grade, then, depends upon either the creation of new positions in an annual budget or the appearance of vacancies by promotion or attrition. Given this highly rigid table of organization, great competition for promotion in rank exists; this is vital to the all-important career of the civil servant.

The statute provides for the possibility of promotion within a corps by competitive examination. However, the almost universal practice is "by choice." That is, the outcome of the competition is determined, often without written examination, by administrative officers. Seniority and merit rating are taken into account. In each case there must be established a promotion table prior to the filling of positions which may become open. The table lists in priority order the civil servants eligible for promotion. Each statute specific to a corps determines which civil servants, by seniority, step, and so forth are eligible to apply for promotion. To apply they request that their names be placed on the table. Before determination as to which applicants to place on the current table, the administrator is required to consult the C.A.P. While the role of the C.A.P. is advisory only, failure to include an applicant, contrary to advice, is appealable to the C.S.F.P., itself a bipartite body charged, among other matters, with general supervision over the C.A.P.

Interviewees inform me that most problems of difference between administrators and the C.A.P. are worked out and agreement reached on the promotion tables. Appeals are virtually unheard of. The strong influence of the trade unions is probably the major factor behind the dominance of the seniority criterion in promotion from grade to grade.

In addition to the promotion function, the C.A.P. are consulted on the conversion to regular civil service status of probationary employees. This, however, does not seem to be a major element of controversy or of function.

The C.A.P. also serve as committees of discipline. The administration is required to consult them prior to rendering serious discipline. Their powers, however, are only advisory. Appeal may also be had to the C.S.F.P., but it can also only advise the administration. However, for municipal employees a bipartite appeals body exists for appeals from local C.A.P. serving as disciplinary committees, and for such employees the action of the appeals committee is binding on the municipality.

An alternative appeals route exists for civil servants. They may go to the administrative courts with appeals against disciplinary action. The court is authorized to judge both the law and the facts of their cases, or to determine whether there was an abuse of administrative authority. Decisions of the administrative courts are binding on the government. Indeed, unlike the ordinary or labor courts in cases involving employees in the private sector, the administrative courts may issue a binding order directing the reinstatement of a dismissed civil servant. Thus the courts can direct the sovereign power to do that which they may not direct a private person to do. This anomaly arises out of the fact that private employees are under contract of personal service which is subject to the French equivalent of the rule that such contracts may not be enforced against either party by specific performance. On the other hand, civil servants in French law occupy a "status" rather than being parties to a contract with the government. Hence the rules of contract do not apply, and the administrative courts have no difficulty in deciding that status illegally removed has not been removed at all.

The civil service statutes provide for a hierarchy of discipline: a warning, a notation in the personnel file of the commission of a breach, removal from the promotion table, reduction of seniority in step, reduction of step, transfer, demotion (in grade), compulsory retirement, dismissal with retention of pension rights, and dismissal without retention of pension rights. All but the first two require consultation of the C.A.P. before being imposed, though in serious cases the civil servant may be suspended pending decision. Given the right of recourse to the administrative courts, relatively few, at least of the serious disciplinary measures, are appealed to the C.S.F.P. I am told that it hears only three or four discipline cases per year. This of course is not the case for the bipartite appeals board for municipal employees, where decisions are binding.

The C.A.P. may also deal with disputes over merit ratings, and problems of leaves, transfers, or any other matters which concern the civil servant as an individual. The trade union plays a double role in proceedings before the C.A.P. First, of course, since most employee members of the C.A.P. are elected from trade union lists, they select candidates and serve, through them, as the representative of employee interests on the C.A.P. Second, they have the right, on request, to represent employees before the C.A.P. Indeed, they may appear in their own interest and that of employees generally. They also perform this representative function in the administrative courts.

The central government civil servant unions are probably the best staffed in France. Hence this characteristic role of representation before bipartite bodies and in the courts is probably better performed by these unions than by any others. Their ability to provide the necessary staff is a result of the willingness of the government, on an informal and extralegal basis, to detach civil servants for union service while continuing to pay them their salaries. I am told that there are several hundred such civil servants working full time in the service of their unions while receiving their governmental pay.

It should be added that this is not the case for the municipal worker unions. There may be communes which permit certain of their paid employees to function as union officials for all or large parts of their time, but it is not general. The federation offices are almost as typically understaffed as are most French unions. Some differences exist because members of these unions probably pay dues with greater regularity than do members of unions in the private sector. The municipal employee unions are known as among the best financed of French unions.

An almost universal judgment of unionists and public administrators is that the C.A.P. work effectively in representing individual civil servant's interests and in dealing with the administration. The view is quite different concerning the C.T.P. The functions of the C.T.P. are to advise the relevant minister or his representative on all matters submitted to it concerning organization, functioning, and personnel policies of the administration, and concerning the development or change in special statutes concerning the corps in the service. The C.T.P. are bipartite. On the employee side, members are named by the trade union organizations found by the minister concerned to be the most representative in the relevant service. The number of seats to be filled by each such "most representative" union is also determined by the minister.

This method of designation may be one of the reasons for the relative failure of the C.T.P.; there have been allegations from certain unions, notably C.G.T., that seats have been inequitably divided. Thus there may be a predisposition of hostility to begin with. Second, in many ministries and services there has been a great reluctance to establish C.T.P., even though they are required by law. While I am unaware of any count of existing C.T.P., I was informed by virtually every interviewee with whom the subject came up that large parts of the civil service are without C.T.P. Undoubtedly, administrators are reluctant to share even advisory authority over such fundamental matters of administration with a bipartite body.

Their fears, however, may be unfounded, since a third factor said to account for the relative failure of the C.T.P. was the insistence of trade union members in those which were established that they deal with problems outside their jurisdiction—either individual problems which lay within the jurisdiction of the C.A.P., or wage and wage structure problems. The experience seems to have been that often the trade union representatives have little interest in the administrative and organizational problems with which the C.T.P. were to deal.

General supervision of the C.A.P. and C.T.P., as well as other functions, is vested in the C.S.F.P. It is a bipartite body with sixteen trade unionists and sixteen designees of the government. The trade union representatives are named by the most representative unions. Government representatives must include certain officers including the budget director and the general director of administration and the civil service.

Currently the trade union representatives include five members from F.O., three from C.G.T., three from the autonomous Fédération de l'Education Nationale, two from C.F.D.T., one from C.F.T.C., and one from C.G.C. Representation of the F.E.N. frequently provokes discussion since its members are limited to a single governmental sector. But it would be impossible to exclude, being by far the largest single organization of government employees. C.G.T. claims that it is seriously underrepresented.

As we have noted, the C.S.F.P. functions as an appeals body for grievances over merit rating and promotion, as well as general supervisor over the C.A.P. and C.T.P. It receives some of these kinds of cases, though its decisions are merely advisory. Where it is able to reach majority decisions, however, it has great authority since the government representatives come from the top echelons. In hearing appeals cases, the C.S.F.P. sits as a whole. It has, however, the additional function of advising the government on all matters pertaining to the civil service that may be submitted to it. When such matters are referred to it, the trade union and government representatives consider the matter in separate sections. If the advice coming from each section is the same, the matter is conveyed to the government as the advice of the C.S.F.P. However, if there are even partial differences, the C.S.F.P. considers the matter as a whole. Such general sessions are presided over by the prime minister, who has a deciding vote in case of a tie.

We have already noted certain aspects of the bipartite structure for municipal employees. For each commune (or group of communes of less than one hundred inhabitants within a department) there is a bipartite commission which performs functions roughly parallel to those of the C.T.P. as well as many of the individual matters considered by the C.A.P. For discipline matters, a special discipline commission is established composed of members from each side of the bipartite commission chosen by lot.[1]

A national bipartite commission for communal employees has also been established, consisting of mayors, some elected by their peers and some named by presidents of associations of mayors and municipalities. In addition, two mayors are named by the minister of the interior. Six employee representatives are elected from lists proposed by groups or unions of employees, and four are named by the most representative unions. Two are named by the minister of the interior.

The national bipartite commission serves as an appeals body on individual grievances, with binding power of decision. In addition, it participates in the establishment of general rules for recruitment, promotion, discipline, and other matters

---

1. As in the case of central government employees, a civil servant may be judged only by those holding his own rank or higher.

concerning the local civil service. It should be noted, however, that in these matters it deals with the national government, generally the minister of the interior, which has the power to establish such rules governing local governments. The General Civil Service Statute for Municipal Employees embodies the general principles, and a large body of decrees serves to implement them. In general they are analogous to the rules for national civil servants. Parallel structures exist for employees of hospitals and other state medical institutions.

·VII·
Summary and Conclusions

IT is a little difficult to arrive at a total assessment of the impact of civil service unionism in France. Part of the problem is in the terms upon which such an assessment is to be made.

First, it is clear that if we are to judge by the standards of successful American-style collective bargaining, whose purpose it is to arrive at binding agreements concerning terms and conditions of employment, unions of public employees in France have accomplished little. On the other hand, staying with the goal of collective bargaining, if the comparison were to be made with the success of private sector unions in France the comparison would be much less devastating. French unions have the right to bargain collectively in the private sector, as they do not in the public, and a network of industry agreements covering much of the private sector have been signed. Yet their influence on wages and conditions of employment is not great; they serve only as minima and actual terms usually exceed those provided in the agreements. Though public unions do not bargain collectively in the strict sense, they probably have no less, though little more, influence on basic terms of employment than do their colleague unions in private industry.

It is not really hard to imagine evolution toward a system of agreed legislation, by statute or decree, which would represent a reasonable adaptation of collective bargaining to the French public service environment. This is undoubtedly what the C.G.T. has in mind when its representatives talk about moving toward a system of collective bargaining. The notion is not strange to a system in which the preferred type of collective agreement itself takes the form of a decree extending an industry-wide agreement to the whole of an industry. The agreements of the spring of 1968 and October 1969 may be significant steps in this direction.

One kind of problem which presents itself to a system

like the American with its strict separation of the executive and legislative branches does not face the French public employee unions. Once access is gained to the government in the person of the prime minister and the minister of finance, they confront the real source of decision in financial and nonfinancial matters, so far as civil servants are concerned. The government budget, under the Fifth Republic, is almost certain to be the budget. This would be the usual case in any parliamentary system. And while the Fifth Republic is some sort of cross between a British-style parliamentary system and an American-style presidential system, the special rules limiting parliamentary control over budgets and the powers of decree held by government in matters not concerning basic law give sufficiently wide discretionary powers to the government so that unions could have access to the proper interlocutor. But their power to influence decisions through that interlocutor appears quite limited.

It is hard to say why so many French civil servants choose to join unions. We know that they do in numbers which are large by comparison with employees of private enterprises, and by comparison with public employees in, say, the United States. Furthermore, this is no new phenomenon in France; public employee unions have been strong and stable for about fifty years.

French civil servants are, however, probably more consciously turned toward the job and its status than the typical French manual worker in industry. In part this comes from his virtual lifetime commitment to a civil service career upon his entry, usually his first or nearly his first job. While the manual worker may be more interested in immediate social and economic goals than his trade union leaders believe, or would like, the civil servant is probably less interested in long range political or revolutionary goals than is the worker in private industry.

If this is so, and I believe it is, then the long-term attachment of large numbers of civil servants to their unions is probably symptomatic of a point of view that some results are achieved by the use of this instrument. We have noted the difficulty of measuring any impact on wages, though there is some quite inconclusive evidence that there has been some such impact, that is, at least that the stronger the civil service union the higher the wage among civil servants. We have described the processes by which there is a periodic major adjustment in wages after a buildup of several years of increasing discontent. Trade unions serve to stimulate and focus this discontent, and toward the end of each cycle they are able to bring pressure by demonstration strikes throughout the public service. Gradual improvements in other economic terms of employment have been gained. No doubt the civil servant attributes some of these wage and economic gains to union action, even though there is no collective bargaining in the accepted sense. But, as we have noted, the process is not terribly different from the traditional one in private industry.

Discussions of general wage changes and large-scale general adjustments in the "grill" take place at annual budget-making time. Discussions of changes in indexes for individual positions or of assigning indexes to new positions go on almost continuously. In them the trade unions play a major direct role at least to the ministerial level. We have noted the intensity of feeling that prevails among civil servants on these issues which involve direct comparisons with other civil servants. It might be supposed that these are matters which attach the allegiance of the civil servant to his union as the principal defender of his relative status in the hierarchy. With his corporate view and his commitment to his career, his relative place in the hierarchy is a very important symbolic expression to the civil servant. Without his union he has little place to turn against the real or imagined deprivation of that status, perhaps by the aggressive efforts of other civil service unions.

The achievement, however, which is probably more important to civil servants than doubtful impacts on statutory wages and working conditions is in the daily activity of their unions working through representatives on the bipartite bodies and by way of representation before them on the individual problems of their careers.

Probably nothing seems more important to the typical civil servant than his success in progressing through the steps within his grade and from grade to grade within his corps. The C.A.P. structure which permits him, through his union, to gain a hearing on his bid for a place on the promotion table, and to question merit ratings which may prejudice his chances for a grade promotion or delay his passage from one step to another, is undoubtedly held as a major union achievement and function. Likewise, the ability to question minor discipline which may deprive him of some of his all-important seniority serves the same purpose. In a crisis the availability of union representation before the administrative courts makes of his union dues a very valuable form of insurance against certain kinds of legal costs. More generally, the role of the unions in protecting the civil service against political interference and of maintaining the independence of the civil servant is one of the great achievements of public service unionism.

Decisions of the C.A.P. or, on appeal, of the C.S.F.P. are merely advisory. Though there are no data, and they would be extremely difficult to obtain, I have been told repeatedly that in such matters as merit rating, promotion tables, and minor discipline the C.A.P. are normally able to come to a decision and that their advice is normally taken by the administration.

Such a result may come as a surprise to those who have been impressed by the "class" or revolutionary formal ideology of the French labor movement and by the fact the C.G.T. is well represented on the C.A.P. Yet in other bipartite French institutions such as the Conseil de Prud'hommes, labor courts having jurisdiction over individual disputes between employers and employees in private industry, on which C.G.T. is even better represented, decisions are reached in virtually all cases without the necessity of intervention of a neutral judge.[1] The only added step in the civil service is the willingness

1. See McPherson and Meyers, *The French Labor Courts.*

of the government to accept what in its case is advice rather than binding decision.

At the corps or service level, the larger function of advice on general organization, supposed to be performed by the C.T.P., seems far less successfully performed. In many services, C.T.P. have not even been organized. There seems to be a mutual disinclination to deal with these matters, if at all, through the statutorily established machinery.

On the more general issues involving a whole ministry or the entire civil service, the government religiously consults the C.S.F.P. I have the impression that the director general of the civil service and the prime minister and his cabinet take that advice quite seriously. They would be reluctant to undertake a major organizational change without the assent of the C.S.F.P., expressed in more unanimous terms than simply the casting of a tie-breaking vote by the prime minister. Some issues, however, break these bounds and become major political problems. Such a one is the proposal under discussion to break up the Ministry of Post, Telephone, and Telegraph and let part of it, perhaps, revert to private hands, to put all or part of it under an autonomous government corporation, or some combination of such alternatives. Under pressure from the unions in the affected ministry, union representatives on C.S.F.P. would be unalterably opposed. Though the government has moved slowly in the discussions, it is not inconceivable that such a step might be taken without consent, since consent to a workable (if, as is argued, the present structure is unworkable) scheme might not be achievable.

It is a little difficult, then, to sum up the impact of public employee unionism in France. It seems clear that it satisfies some need of the civil servant, since he is unusually loyal to his union. It may have had some impact on economic terms of employment, despite the difficult series of filters through which the trade union must pass before it becomes effective. Only in crisis situations such as that of the late spring of 1968 can that impact be really identified; even then it was part of a large-scale social movement. That movement was in significant part responsible for the ensuing economic and budgetary crisis in France, leading to the devaluation of the franc. But outside such a very rare crisis, the effect of union pressures on wages cannot be so identified as to lead in turn to identification of their effect on general budget policies.

Determination of conditions of employment of civil servants in France is, as elsewhere, a part of the general political process. In the past, particularly during the twenties, the civil service unions were actively engaged in lobbying and election activities, the latter especially at the local level. But since the "great victories" of 1946 and 1953 leading to the enactment of the General Civil Service Statutes for national and local employees, and since the enactment of the postwar constitutions giving Parlement less direct influence, civil service unions, like others, have and do engage in politics, though they refrain, in accordance with the French tradition, from formal connections with political parties. The latter statement means something less for C.G.T.-affiliated unions than it does for others, though there is no formal relation between C.G.T. and the French Communist Party. But their political positions are more likely to be aligned to the general positions of the confederations to which they are affiliated than to positions special to the civil service. Their important tactic, however, is less parliamentary and electoral activity than direct action in the form of demonstration strikes. This also is in the French trade union tradition.

Learning lessons from other countries in the form of adopting intact particular institutions is a dangerous process. Institutions perform as they do because of their environmental context. As I and a colleague have said elsewhere: "The comparative study of industrial relations systems and institutions leads to better understanding of the systems and may, as a byproduct, suggest new or altered policies. But these policies can seldom be merely imitative."[2]

As to the subject matter of this essay, it is more than apparent that there is little about the French system that

2. McPherson and Meyers, *The French Labor Courts,* p. 98.

can be imitated in the U. S. The whole political structure and environment and that of the civil service, not to speak of the general system of industrial relations, are so different that they require different institutions and produce quite different organizational responses. To the scholar, much of interest can be learned as to the reasons for the kinds of responses produced by different kinds of environments. But to the institution builder, there is, in my opinion, little in the French experience that is immediately suggestive of answers to U. S. problems of relations between the state as employer and organizations of public employees.